What does a **GREAT LIFE** look like?

A Great Life Now: The Journey to a Life with Less Stress and More Optimism, Happiness, & Success

Published by Brand At Work

Editor: Courtney Cooley, Mar Rel Editing Services

Copy editor: Sarah J. Singer Editing Services

Cover art and interior layout design: Heidi Sutherlin, My Creative Pursuits

ISBN: 978-0-9795875-7-3

"Once you have **self worth,** you can move **mountains.**"

~ Carol Lederman

Message from the author
+ dedication to you

I'm immensely grateful this book found its way into your hands. My sincere hope is that it sparks deep thought into who you are, where you are going, and how you will get there... and helps you to fully express your gifts, talents, and desires for success in the future. *A Great Life NOW* is based on personal development methods I've practiced and taught to successful leaders in business and in life—from CEOs and their leadership teams to everyday, kind-hearted, and highly motivated souls.

I considered writing this book for more than a decade but could not find the time as I was fully consumed with running my company, ensuring I spent time with family, and fulfilling a hectic schedule of client engagements and speeches. However, everywhere around me, I continued to see people in need of personal transformation to overcome the social, mental, physical and nutritional deficiencies that plagued them. I saw that people want simple to understand and easy to implement exercises, tools, and techniques that allow them to take charge of life and design and lead it the way they know it should be.

First, I wrote *The Great Life NOW Journey*, a three- to twelve-month curriculum designed to radically transform the way a human thinks, speaks, and acts in this game of life.

Then I wrote this book.

The version of *A Great Life NOW* that you hold in your hands is a small component in the journey. I struggled with determining what the right amount of content should be. I didn't want to go so deep that you, as a reader, feel like you're drinking from a fire hose (and too overwhelmed to actually do anything), while also making sure that those who want to can take the time to focus and dive into the thoughtful exercises in order to gain tremendous insight and transform how they see the world and themselves in it. I even second-guessed whether to create this condensed version of the journey at all, knowing that it's only the tip of the iceberg.

However, after quite a bit of deliberation, I followed my heart. I took the leap, knowing that this book has the opportunity to positively influence many more lives than I could ever reach from the speaking stage or in a coaching relationship.

I've given all that I have in writing this book for you. I am inspired by the great majority of people who want a greater life than they are living now. I am grateful that you are embracing this and therefore dedicate this book to you: the reader who is motivated to take the journey through this great game of life.

The world needs more happy, healthy, and successful people. Why wait for more of them? Why not just become one of them? Starting today. Beginning NOW!

With gratitude + love,

Gregg

If you asked 1,000 different people what a great life looks like, you would NOT get 1,000 different answers. In fact, you wouldn't even get 100 different answers. You'd fin that certain answers show up on most people's lists.

Most would agree that living a great life includes living with a sense of purpose, having fun, and having an energy and focus that leads to less stress and more time to do the things you love, with the people you love. Most would agree it doesn't mean *having* more—more stuff, more money, more prestige—it means *being* more.

More courageous. **More loving.** Happier.

All of this is achievable right NOW.
And that is what this book is all about.

Life is a game.

Life is a game like all other games. The good news is... you get to make up your own set of rules for this game.

Those rules are your **VALUES**.

Whether consciously or unconsciously, these rules are based on your beliefs, and they dramatically impact the habits you put in place for how you play the game.

You need a Game Plan.

The Great Life Now journey provides you the opportunity to create your Game Plan. First, you'll get warmed up with some Pro Game thinking, then you'll create your plan, and finally you'll

ACTIVATE it.

A Great Life
NOW...

...doesn't happen

by CHANCE

... it happens by design.

NOW
is the time.

This is your life, the only life you get, and you should make the most of it by designing it the way you want it. Doing so will optimize your happiness and success.

WHY?

Because life is HAPPENING right NOW!

We all have two choices: We can make a living or **we can design a life**.

~ Jim Rohn

A small amount of effort is needed to make your life Great NOW. About 3% of your time.

You get the same 1,440 minutes each day that everyone else does.

Assume you sleep eight hours a day. That leaves 16 hours of awake time for work and personal activities: **960 minutes.**

$$16 \text{ hours awake}$$
$$\times 60 \text{ minutes per hour}$$
$$\overline{960} \text{ minutes each day}$$

QUESTION:

Will you invest **3%** of your day to ensure the other **97%** is truly Great?

READ ON to learn how ...

If you fail to plan,
you are planning to fail

~ Ben Franklin

PRE-GAME

How **many days** do you have left?

Consider that the average life expectancy for someone in the U.S. is 78.6 years.

EXAMPLE BASED ON A 38-YEAR-OLD

38 X 365 = 13,870 days old
(average age in U.S.) X (days in year) =
(average # of days old)

Average life expectancy =
78.6 years or 28,689 days

28,689 - 13,870 = 14,819 days left

Take diseases, illnesses, and accidents off the table and think about a realistic age for you to live to.

Fill in the equation below to figure out your days.

How many days old are you?

_____ X 365 = _____

(your age) X (days in a year) = (# of days old)

How many days do you have in total?

_____ X 365 = _____

(life expectancy) X (days in a year) = (total days)

How many days do you have left?

_____ - _____ = _____

(total days) - (# of days old) = (days left)

Where are you **NOW** on the **Pathway of Life?**

The Pathway of Life is sequential from birth to death and captures a high-level view of where you've been and, most importantly, where you are going next in your journey to a Great Life NOW.

Your life can be divided into three big phases with two fluctuations between them. The fluctuations represent a period of about 10 years where new milestones are achieved.

As you evolve through each phase, you become physically, mentally, and circumstantially a very different person. But you may not even notice these changes as they tend to blend together.

Read on to learn more about each phase.

The Pathway of Life

SAVORING
Phase 3

Death

RESPONSIBILITY
Phase 2

flux

SHAPING
Phase 1

flux

Birth

Phase 1: Shaping

You're completely dependent on others as you learn and grow. Parents, teachers, coaches, and friends are guiding, influencing, and molding you into a young adult. You start with very little freedom of choice; however, it grows over time.

Your teenage years bring the first of two fluctuation points (flux) where a shift in personality, priorities, stress level, and choices takes place. This flux typically includes milestones such as graduating from school and entering the full-time work world. A significant shift in accountability for choices takes place and you most likely became much less dependent on others.

Phase 2: Responsibility

Others are dependent on you as you work to provide for yourself and your family. Your personality and work ethic have developed, but you still have a need for personal development and growth. This phase can be adventurous, packed with newfound freedom to make life-altering choices (such as where to live, what to do for work, and who to spend time with), but you may also find that you're taking on more stress and burden.

The Responsibility phase is packed with many difficult choices, which makes it critical for you to be able to prioritize your energy and focus to make optimal decisions. (The kind of decisions that make for a Great Life NOW.) Those who cannot prioritize become overwhelmed and struggle to find balance, harmony, and joy at this stage of life.

Phase 3: Savoring

Fewer big decisions, fewer responsibilities, less daily stress... in most cases, it's the complete opposite of the Responsibility phase. Different challenges, such as health issues and a lack of belonging tend to increase during this phase. However, others are no longer dependent on you and you may no longer have to work, or at least you can work less.

The fluctuation years between Responsibility and Savoring may lead to many transitions depending on your desire to keep working, your physical, mental, and financial well-being, and the relationships you have in your life. When you create and activate your Great Life NOW Game Plan, you'll increase the probability of having more choices in the way you transition into phase three.

Once you get there, you'll find you are free to enjoy life with more desirable levels of flexibility. You are savoring life. You earned it!

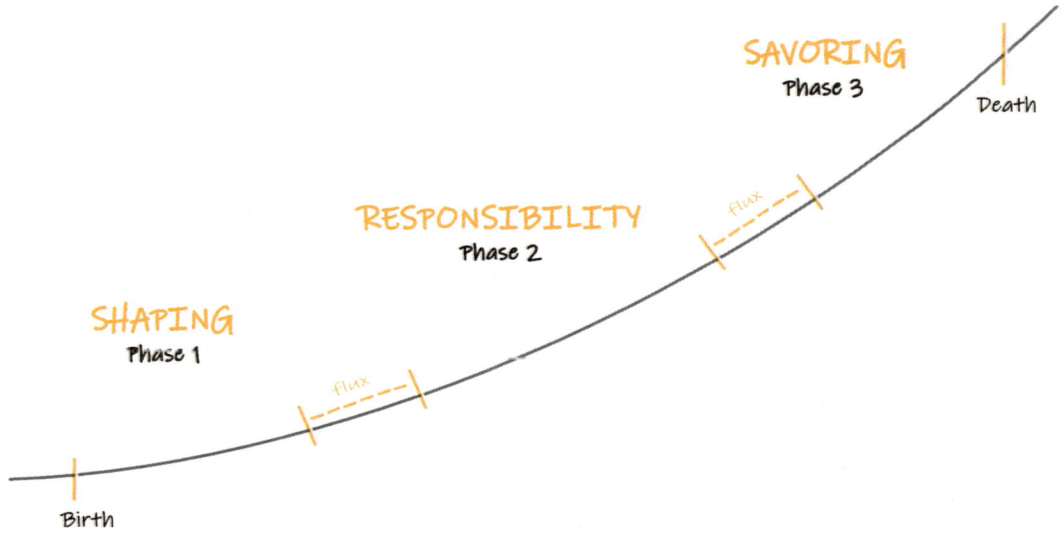

On the following page, reflect on where you are and where you are going as you move through your Pathway of Life.

FILL IN YOUR
PATHWAY

1. Draw a stick figure of where you are on the Pathway of Life.

2. Backfill important choices and milestones you've experienced along the way to where you are now (e.g., graduations, relationships, jobs, wedding, etc.)

3. Think about the next 5, 10, or 15 years. What are the goals and milestones you'd like to achieve along the way?

Goals & Milestones

....

....

....

....

....

....

SHAPING
Phase 1

flux

Birth

Your Pathway of Life

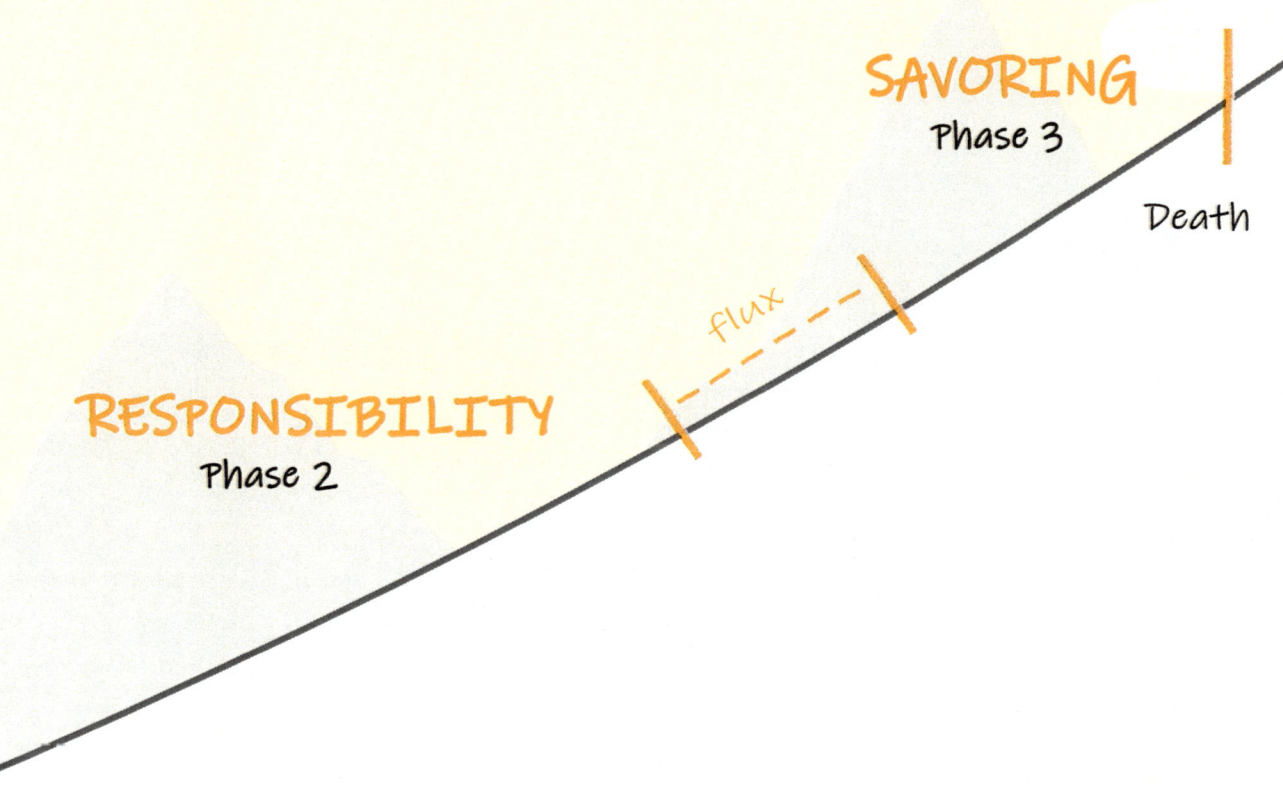

SAVORING
Phase 3

Death

flux

RESPONSIBILITY
Phase 2

NOW's the time **to get o~**

Someday Island.

How do you know if you're on it? Well, for example, if you have ideas or ambitions you want to accomplish but keep giving excuses for not taking action, then you are most likely on Someday Island.

Many people on Someday Island feel they will be happy later when something else happens: *"Someday I'll do this and be happy. Someday I'll do that and be happy."*

The reality is, Someday never comes. Unless you muster up the courage and motivation to take action.

What have you **told** yourself?

Circle and add to the list.

I'll be happy when ...

- I find that mate.
- I buy that car.
- I hire another employee.
- I close that deal.
- I have that skill.
- I lose that weight.
- I have the time.
- I make more money.
- I quit this job.
- I have that baby.
- I eat that _____.
- _____
- _____
- _____
- _____

Your time to **take action** is NOW.

You can't acquire your way to happiness.

Let's say you live on Someday Island thinking you will be happier once you earn a certain amount of money to secure your future. So, you put all your energy into work and your career. and after years of body-depleting stress, broken relationships, and constant personal sacrifi es. you make millions of dollars.

Uh-oh. Do you know where this is going?

Did you achieve your goal of making a lot of money? YES!

Did you reach your desired level of happiness? NO!

AN INSIDE JOB.

Happiness is not outcome dependent. It won't come from making more money, getting a better job, driving a fancier car, achieving a certain body weight, or findin the perfect mate.

You'll discover (or rediscover) that happiness really is an inside job—and once you do, you'll be able to think and act with more purpose, confiden e, optimism, creativity, and decisiveness than ever before.

You will clearly see that happiness is right here, right **NOW**… and, in doing so, you will drop the illusion that happiness exists on the other side of any place, possession, person, or achievement.

Success is **not** the key to happiness. It's the other way around.

Happiness is the key to success.

Happiness
is the purpose of life.

HAPPY people benefit from:

Stronger immune systems

More fulfilling and longer-lasting marriages

Fewer heart attacks and strokes

Larger, more active social lives

More involvement within their communities

Less pain and inflammation

More resilient personalities able to handle adversity better

Living longer

Happiness is a choice & you control that choice.

A few lies we tell ourselves about happiness...

Lie #1: My genetics determine my happiness.

Yes, happiness is hereditary, but only up to a point. Research tells us that 50% of happiness comes from our genetic makeup. Therefore, just because your mom or dad chose to be miserable and unhappy doesn't mean you have to. Those cards you've been dealt only make up half your hand.

Lie #2: My life circumstances are a primary driver of my happiness.

Only about 10% of our happiness is circumstantial, meaning only a fraction is influen ed by differences in life situations such as whether you are rich or poor, healthy or unhealthy, beautiful or more ordinary looking, married or divorced, etc.

Lie #3: I can't control my happiness.

40% of our happiness is within our control. You can increase or decrease your happiness based on how you think, speak, and act in your daily life.

Don't fall victim to the **LIES.**

The most important CHOICE of your life.

Once you make the CHOICE, your journey through life can be a Great one, right NOW.

HAPPY people:

- Invest their time with family and friends. They are committed to nurturing those relationships.

- Practice gratitude.

- Give to others. They are typically the first to offer a helping hand.

- Are optimistic when imagining their future.

- Focus their energy on living in the present.

- Exercise habitually.

- Have ambitions and goals and are committed to achieving them.

- Remain poised and courageous when facing life's challenges and setbacks.

Will you choose to be HAPPY?

Happiness is . . .

· to want what you HAVE . . .

while you pursue what you WANT . . .

WHAT HAPPINESS LOOKS LIKE

"Happiness comes in waves ... you'll find it again." "When you love what you have, you'll have everything you need." "Happiness is letting go of what you think your life is supposed to look like." "Want to be happy? When it rains, look for rainbows, when it's dark, look for stars." "The happiness of your life depends on the quality of your thoughts." "You deserve to be happy. You deserve to live a life you are excited about. Don't let others make you forget that." "Happiness comes when we stop complaining about the troubles we have and offer thanks for all the troubles we don't have." "The most important thing is to enjoy your life - to be happy. It's all that matters." - Audrey Hepburn "The purpose of our life is to be happy." "Happiness is the best makeup" - Drew Barrymore "I think you should enjoy every minute of it." - Meghan Markle "The mere sense of living is joy enough." - Emily Dickinson "If you want to be happy, be." - Leo Tolstoy "The only thing that will make you happy is being happy with who you are, and not who people think you are." "Most folks are as happy as they make up their minds to be." - Abraham Lincoln "Simplicity makes me happy." "Independence is happiness." - Susan B. Anthony "Happiness cannot be traveled to, owned, earned, or worn. Happiness is the spiritual experience of living every minute with love, grace, and gratitude." - Denis Waitley "Spread love everywhere you go. Let no one ever come without leaving happier." - Mother Teresa "Happiness is not something you postpone for the future; it is something you design for the present." - Jim Rohn "There is only one happiness in this life: to love and to be loved." - George Sand "Happiness is a choice. You can choose to be happy. There's going to be stress in life, but it's your choice whether you let it affect you or not." - Valerie Bertinelli "Happiness never decreases by being shared." - Buddha "When one door of happiness closes, another opens; but often we look so long at the closed door that we do not see the one which has opened for us." - Helen Keller "Happiness doesn't depend on any external conditions, it is governed by our mental attitude." - Dale Carnegie "The key to being happy is knowing you have the power to choose what to accept and what to let go." - Dodinsky

what areas of your life
are you happy about?

why are you happy with
these areas of your life?

what is one thing you
are not happy with?

why are you not happy
with this one thing?

what might you consider doing differently in
the future that will bring you more happiness?

The only
thing we
have to
FEAR
is fear itself.

~ Franklin Delano Roosevelt

FACE YOUR
F.E.

99%

or more of the fears

we stimulate inside

ourselves never

come to pass.

As opposed to early humans who needed to protect themselves from physical harm caused by wild animals or other humans, nearly all our fears today are non-physical. They exist only in our heads, such as fearing people or places, or emotional insecurities.

YOU can stop letting fear control your thinking and negatively impact your stress level and happiness.

F.E.A.R.

False Evidence Appearing Real

What were your **biggest** worries ...

6 months ago?	1 year ago?	5 years ago?
· · · · · · · · · · · ·	· · · · · · · · · · · ·	· · · · · · · · · · · ·
· · · · · · · · · · · ·	· · · · · · · · · · · ·	· · · · · · · · · · · ·
· · · · · · · · · · · ·	· · · · · · · · · · · ·	· · · · · · · · · · · ·
· · · · · · · · · · · ·	· · · · · · · · · · · ·	· · · · · · · · · · · ·
· · · · · · · · · · · ·	· · · · · · · · · · · ·	· · · · · · · · · · · ·
· · · · · · · · · · · ·	· · · · · · · · · · · ·	· · · · · · · · · · · ·
· · · · · · · · · · · ·	· · · · · · · · · · · ·	· · · · · · · · · · · ·
· · · · · · · · · · · ·	· · · · · · · · · · · ·	· · · · · · · · · · · ·
· · · · · · · · · · · ·	· · · · · · · · · · · ·	· · · · · · · · · · · ·
· · · · · · · · · · · ·	· · · · · · · · · · · ·	· · · · · · · · · · · ·
· · · · · · · · · · · ·	· · · · · · · · · · · ·	· · · · · · · · · · · ·

How many of these **worries** have materialized in your life?

If you stop
worrying
about what

might

happen
tomorrow,
you're free
to enjoy
more of
TODAY.

EXPLORING YOUR FEARS

Get your fears out in the open where you can decide to either crush them or recognize they exist and will continue to get in your way.

1. List your biggest fears. Think about what keeps you up at night. Are there specifi worries you consistently have? Do you have any fears that may be "hiding" on you that you could spot after some reflection

2. For each fear, determine how it has served you in your life. What are the benefit you get from that fear?

3. What might the fear be costing you? Why should you consider letting it go… freeing yourself?

4. What thoughts or actions would lessen the fear? What mantra or saying could you tell yourself that would alleviate the fear?

1.
What are your greatest fears?

Example

Fear of failure

2.
What benefit has the fear given you in the past?

Motivated me to work very hard, long hours for over 20 years.

3.

Why free yourself of the fear now?

I have way too much stress, which decreases my happiness and makes me less successful at work and at home.

4.

How can you free yourself (thoughts or actions)?

Daily hour of power each morning w/15 mins meditation.

Review family & personal values each day.

"Nothing to prove, everything to share."

May your *Choices* **reflect** *your* *Hopes,* **not your** *Fears.*

~ Nelson Mandela

You've evaluated your life through the three phases of the Pathway, uncovered what happiness looks like, and explored your fears.

Phew... that's a lot.

Next, you'll dive into designing your

Great Life NOW Game Plan.

> We are what we
> repeatedly do.
>
> ~ Aristotle

GAME PLAN

Let your passion fuel your purpose.

Uncovering your passion(s) will help you live "on purpose," shaping your character and playing a signifi ant role in ensuring you live a Great Life NOW.

What are you PASSIONATE ABOUT?

Think about activities you do at work, with your family, or in your community. Consider hobbies, sports, or any combination.

I'm PASSIONATE about:

....

....

....

....

....

....

....

....

....

EXAMPLES:

- Cooking a meal for a group of freinds

- Helping a customer solve a problem

- Collaborating on a project with coworkers

- Taking a weekend trip with your kid

- Presenting your idea in a meeting

Let your passion

What's your purpose?
Some questions to get you thinking.

What do you most value in life?

When you were a child, what did you want to be when you got older? Why?
What was the feeling you wanted to have?

When you were a child, who was your role model? What did you admire about them?

Think of a situation in your life when things were really flowing. You were "in the zone" (also called the "flow state"). Step into that situation again.

- What were you doing?

- What were you feeling?

- Were you learning or doing something interesting?

- Is there anything similar between this time of your life and when you were young?

- What were you creating? Sharing? Feeling?

Take your ideas and insights and write **one inspiring** **Purpose**.

A helpful framework is to include both the activity you do and the results you achieve (for example: "My purpose is to **activity with result(s)**," or, "My purpose is to **result through activity**").

Examples

My purpose is to help people solve problems to live a better life.

My purpose is to raise happy and healthy kids who make a positive difference in the world.

My purpose is to share knowledge and experience to help others grow and succeed.

My purpose is to achieve economic freedom by becoming a sought-after expert in my field.

Have you ever noticed that time   ies when you're doing activities you enjoy, are good at, or that come naturally to you? Hours pass in what feels like minutes because you are doing something that utilizes your unique gifts and talents. You find you're operating at a deeper level, with more energy and enthusiasm, which aligns with your Purpose and leads to greater levels of achievement. This is what happens when you use the traits, skills, talents, and knowledge that make up your Strengths.

Using your Strengths doesn't just benefit you. It also benefits the people you work or interact with. Knowing your Strengths is critical in the discovery of who you are and positions you to achieve more clarity, focus, and success on **your Great Life NOW journey.**

Exploring your Strengths

What are you naturally good at? (You know, the things that come easily, that just feel second nature to you.)

What do you enjoy doing at work, that's not part of your job description, that you just take on without anyone asking you to?

What knowledge and skills have you built in your career that you find valuable?

What tends to be your role with friends and family?

Everything you just listed provides insight into your Strengths—what you're naturally good at. Knowing your Strengths is the first step to uncovering your Superpowers.

Your Superpowers are your top Strengths. By using these Superpowers, you'll be doing more of what you are good at and ultimately will get more of what you want...

... which is a Great Life NOW with less stress and fear and more happiness, optimism, and success.

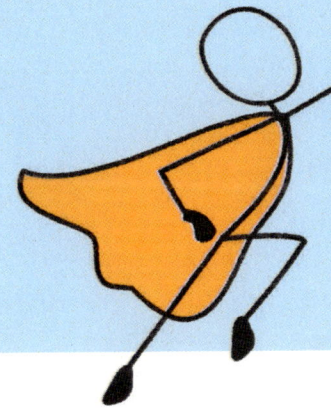

Knowing your Superpower Changes EVERYTHING.

~ Nadalie Bardo

Your Superpowers

1. ....

2. ....

3. ....

A professor stood before his philosophy class with some items in front of him.

When the class began, he said, "We all have this one life to live. A fle ting shadow against all that exists in this vast universe. We have the ability to accomplish anything. Truly anything. If we use our time wisely." He then put a large, empty pickle jar on the desk and, without a word, proceeded to fil it with golf balls.

He then asked the students if the jar was full. They agreed that it was.

So, the professor then picked up a box of pebbles and poured them into the jar. He shook the jar lightly, and the pebbles rolled into the open areas between the golf balls.

He again asked the students if the jar was full.

They agreed it was.

The professor picked up a box of sand and poured it into the jar. Of course, the sand fille up every remaining space.

He asked once more if the jar was full.

The students responded with a unanimous yes.

The professor then produced two cans of beer from under the table and poured the entire contents into the jar, effectively fillin the empty spaces between the grains of sand.

The students laughed.

"Now," said the professor, as the laughter subsided, "I want you to recognize that this jar represents your life. **The golf balls are the important things**—your family, your children, your health, your friends, your favorite passions—things that if everything else was lost and only they remained, your life would still be full. **The pebbles are the other things that matter** like your job, your house, your car. **The sand is everything else**—the small stuff."

"If you put the sand into the jar fi st," he continued, "there is no room for the pebbles or the golf balls. The same goes for life. If you spend all your time and energy on the small stuff, you will never have room for the things that are important to you. Pay attention to the things that are critical to your happiness. Play with your children. Take time to get medical checkups. Take your partner out to dinner. Play another 18. There will always be time to clean the house and fi the disposal. **Take care of the golf balls fi st, the things that really matter. Set your priorities. The rest is just sand.**"

One of the students raised his hand and inquired what the beer represented.

The professor smiled.

"I'm glad you asked," he said. "It just goes to show you that no matter how full your life may seem, there's always room for a couple of beers with friends."

Source: YouTube - Amazingly Simple Theory for Life

BE grateful

Gratitude is the greatest virtue of all as it enables us to connect with something that is not only larger than ourselves but also profoundly good and comforting.

Demonstrating gratitude opens your eyes to the miracles in life and positively influen es your attitude—leading to less stress and more optimism, enthusiasm, and joy while also enabling tranquility, empathy, and greater consciousness.

Stop and view your life through the eyes of the other seven billion people on Earth. Is it not true that billions of them would gladly trade places with you right now?

In fact, is it not true that most of them would be overjoyed to do so?

Be grateful NOW

People you are grateful for:

Things you are grateful for:

Circumstances you are grateful for:

Your values are your rules
for the game of life.

Your values POWER

The Brand Called YOU

How you live your values determines your reputation among family, friends, colleagues, and anyone else you interact with. This is your brand—The Brand Called YOU.

When you are living a Great Life NOW, you are winning consistently. Why? Because like any game, there are rules, and...

YOU GET TO **MAKE UP THE RULES!**

Your values are the rules by which the game of life is played. Identifying your values is a deeply personal exercise about uncovering what is most important to you. Your values are the sacred guidelines that, when followed, bring immense satisfaction, optimism, and meaning to your life.

Everyone has values.

Your values should align with your **Purpose**, leverage your **Superpowers**, and come to life in how you **think, speak, and act**.

She remembered who she was
and the game changed. ~ Lalah Delia

WHO are you?

List your values and explain in a few sentences
why living them every day is important to you.

My Core Values: Why they are important:

You can't
talk your way out
of something you
behaved your way into.
You must
behave your way out.

When you honestly define your values, state them as the rules of the game, and then play by those rules, you are truly living your brand and living a Great Life.

HOW do you live your **values**?

List Continue, Stop, Start activities.

On your best day, how do you demonstrate your values?

(What should you **CONTINUE** doing?)

What things do you do that are out of alignment with your values?

(What should you **STOP** doing?)

What can you begin doing or do more consistently to bring your values to life?

(You guessed it ... what should you **START** doing?)

Happiness is when what we think, what we say, and what we do are in HARMONY

~ Mahatma Gandhi

To make sure you're living a Great Life NOW, you'll want to get laser-focused on the areas in your life where you have the best opportunities to grow.

No matter how accomplished or happy you are, you most likely have areas of your life that could use some improvement—and in many cases, different amounts of improvement.

Don't "GO" through life, GROW through life.

~ Eric Butterworth

There are seven areas for you to focus on. They are your Mountains for Growth™.

Your Mountains for GROWTH

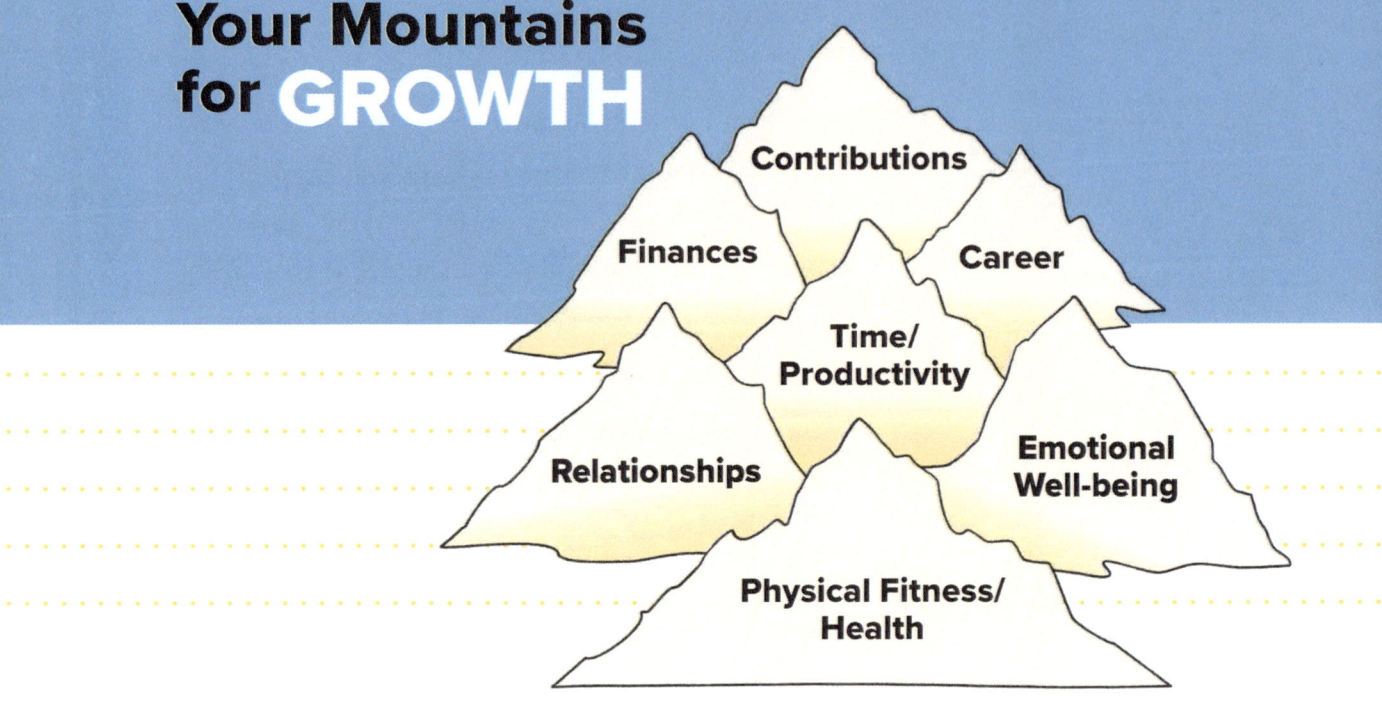

The progress you make "moving your mountains" (i.e., moving forward in each growth area) will help create a more balanced life and fuel the Great Life NOW outcomes you desire: less stress, increased optimism, and more happiness and success. Each mountain has an impact on the others. When you struggle in one area, it can cause suffering in another.

Consider the example of your physical health. Have you reached the peak of your mountain with respect to physical fitness, feeling energetic and full of vitality? If not, consider the impact this has on your emotional well-being or productivity. It may be difficult to move your emotional mountain if you are consistently suffering physically.

If you've reached the mountain peak for physical fitness and health, congratulations! But now move on to another area. Are you highly satisfied with your relationships with family and friends? How about your finances? Are you on the right track to achieve financial freedom? What about your career? Does your job feel like a JOB, that is, something you go to every day to earn income, or is it more of a mission, something you enjoy going to because you feel respected and feel as if you have a positive impact on the lives of others?

The Great Life NOW Mountains for Growth is a simple, easy, and effective way to look at seven main areas of your life and rate how well you are doing so you can decide which mountains you should most focus on for improvement. When evaluating each area, consider your **Core Values**, your **Purpose**, and the **Strengths** and **Superpowers** you can bring to life.

While all seven mountains are important, there is a hierarchy that leads to a level of success and happiness that translates into a Great Life NOW. For example, if you don't master your **Physical Fitness/Health**, then your capacity to maximize your energy is compromised—you might suffer chronic illness or die early. All the money in the world, career success, and contributions to your community will be worthless if you aren't here to enjoy it. You can't experience a Great Life NOW without the vehicle that will help get you them.

Or, if you spend all your energy and time trying to solve your **Relationship** problems, but are not optimizing your **Emotional Well-being**, you will always be at the mercy of life's challenges. Having a fir   handle on your emotions, feeling as if you are in control of the chatter in your mind, frees you to be proactive rather than reactive to challenges and opportunities as they arise.

At the same time, it doesn't make sense to put all your energy and focus into your financial success while shortchanging relationships. What is the point of becoming rich if you end up with a fractured family and very few friends?

Similarly, once you've improved how to **Productively Spend Your Time**, you increase your chances of **Career** success. Once you've made progress to improve your career, you can enhance the chances of growing your **Finances** and improve your ability to give back time and money (**Contributions**) to the people and causes that are most important to you.

This does not mean that you can't work on your finances and improving your health at the same time. **Rather, it shows the importance and hierarchy of the Mountains for Growth—the seven areas to focus on to achieve a Great Life NOW.**

FOCUS AND GROW

1. For each mountain, rate where you are today.

2. Reflect on why you gave yourself that score. What factors did you consider?

3. Document where you want to be. What does a 10 look like to you?

Start thinking about what it would take to move your mountains . . .

YOUR MOUNTAINS

Physical Fitness/Health
Where are you now?

Emotional Well-being
Where are you now?

Relationships
Where are you now?

Time/Productivity
Where are you now?

Career
Where are you now?

Finances
Where are you now?

Contributions
Where are you now?

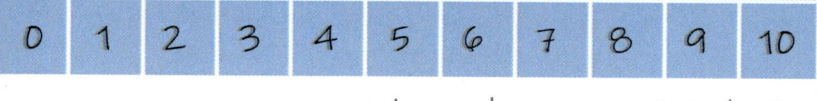

for GROWTH

| 0 | 1 | 2 | 3 | 4 | 5 | 6 | 7 | 8 | 9 | 10 |

where do you want to be?

| 0 | 1 | 2 | 3 | 4 | 5 | 6 | 7 | 8 | 9 | 10 |

where do you want to be?

| 0 | 1 | 2 | 3 | 4 | 5 | 6 | 7 | 8 | 9 | 10 |

where do you want to be?

| 0 | 1 | 2 | 3 | 4 | 5 | 6 | 7 | 8 | 9 | 10 |

where do you want to be?

| 0 | 1 | 2 | 3 | 4 | 5 | 6 | 7 | 8 | 9 | 10 |

where do you want to be?

| 0 | 1 | 2 | 3 | 4 | 5 | 6 | 7 | 8 | 9 | 10 |

where do you want to be?

| 0 | 1 | 2 | 3 | 4 | 5 | 6 | 7 | 8 | 9 | 10 |

where do you want to be?

If it's to
BE,
it's up to
ME.

~ Tim Vottis

The universe rewards
attitude and action.

ACTIVATE

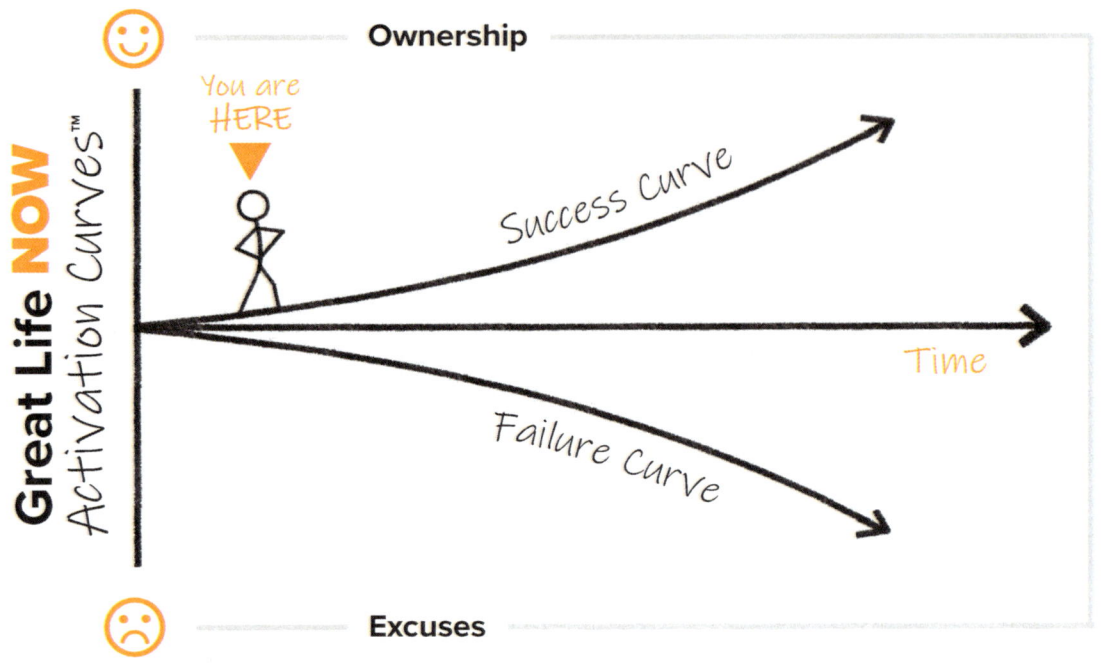

To implement your Great Life NOW Game Plan requires activation of the beliefs, goals, and habits that will positively impact your life.

The Activation Curves reflect your mindset and which direction you are headed.

Those on the Success Curve have a mindset of **ownership** and remain focused and disciplined, while the dominant mindset for those on the Failure Curve is housed in **excuses** for why they could not make the necessary, positive changes in their lives.

You can go one of two directions on the Great Life NOW Activation Curves™:

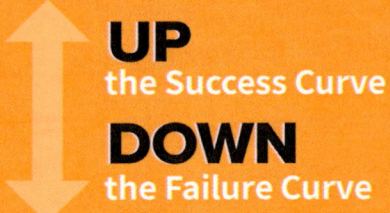

UP the Success Curve
DOWN the Failure Curve

Life is like riding a bicycle...

... you are either moving forward, improving in your areas for growth, or standing still and falling off. You either experience positive momentum up the Success Curve or fall back on the Failure Curve. If you are not improving, enriching, and creating, then you are either running in place, or worse, stepping backward as a human.

If you find yourself on the Failure Curve (and everyone does at times), you don't have to stay there. Now is the time to take action to activate your game plan by building the beliefs, goals, and habits to grow and achieve success in each of the seven areas of the Great Life **NOW** Mountains for Growth.

And the only thing that can get in your way is your mindset.

Your
MINDSET
will get you on

the Success Curve.

QUESTION

What is the one thing you have complete control over in your life?

ANSWER

What you think about.

The greatest discovery of my generation is that a human being can alter his life by altering his attitudes of mind.

~ William James
(American philosopher, 1842-1910)

Everywhere
Everywhere
Everywhere
Negativity is
Everywhere
Everywhere
Everywhere

Don't let it in.

CHOOSE *positive*

Three Strategies to Choose MORE Positivity

1. **Be intentional with how you start your day.**

Avoid beginning your day with negativity. Consider avoiding the news or at least counter it with something positive such as exercise, meditation, or reading or listening to something inspiring.

2. **Be selective about who you spend your time with and who you give your energy and attention to.**

Choose positive people over negative in your friend groups, with your family (when possible), and in who you follow on social media. Listen to the opinions and advice of people you admire. Not simply like, but admire and respect for their accomplishments, integrity, work ethic, or because they truly care about you and what you care about.

3. **Be aware of what content you consume.**

What music do you listen to? What movies and TV shows do you watch? What books, magazines, blogs, and articles do you read? Does this content inspire you, make you feel confident and smart, or at least leave you in a good mood? Or does it instill fear and worry, and leave you with toxic, negative thoughts?

Commit to Consuming
Positivity

What are the **POSITIVE** things you listen to, read, and watch during the day?

What are the **NEGATIVE** things you listen to, read, and watch during the day?

In what ways can you enhance your approach to consuming information and entertainment?

Move from
Scarcity to **Abundance**

Every step of your Great Life NOW journey thus far has positioned you to make a shift in mindset from scarcity to abundance. These two modes of thinking are vastly different, and your success living a Great Life NOW depends, in part, on which mindset you adopt.

A mindset of scarcity is when you focus, usually unconsciously, on what is lacking or wrong in your life. For example, those living on Someday Island tend to think, "I'll be happy when, "which keeps them in a constant mode of scarcity. A scarcity mindset puts you in a place of continual worry, anxiety, fear, and insecurity, and you tend to blame other people or your circumstances for your reality.

Scarcity comes in two forms. One is flight, in which we seek to protect ourselves from an unsafe world by retreating into a comfort zone to avoid failure and rejection. When you are in "flight," you play it safe and avoid competing for fear of losing. The second form of scarcity is to fight for more success. "Fight" is seeking to "win" at life by achieving more and accumulating more, whether in the form of power, status, money, or things. When you're in the "fight" form of scarcity, you're trying to win at life and don't realize that, in most cases, you're only competing against yourself.

Abundance thinkers focus
on what is "**right**" in life.

On the other hand, those who primarily operate with the mindset of abundance more often predict and create their own reality on the Success Curve to goal achievement.

Choosing the abundance mode of thinking means focusing on what is right in life. You see the positivity in most situations, focusing on what is or what could be rather than what is not, what is missing, or what is lacking.

In abundance mode, you are not being unrealistic, you are being realistically positive. When in this mode, you'll still experience negative emotions, thoughts, and situations; however, you will simply choose not to remain in a negative mindset or situation. Abundance thinkers maintain a faith that things happen for a reason and that good will come about.

Abundance thinkers realize that they need to crush their fears, leverage their strengths, and work daily to bring their values to life.

You don't become what you want,
you become what you believe.

~ Oprah Winfrey

The number one difference between the scarcity

Activate
Empowering Beliefs

and abundance thinkers is how they manage their beliefs.

Our beliefs are strong feelings of certainty. They are ideas we hold to be true, regardless of empirical evidence.

Empowering Beliefs are critical to getting on and staying on the Success Curve as they are a primary ingredient that influences your behaviors, goals, and habits.

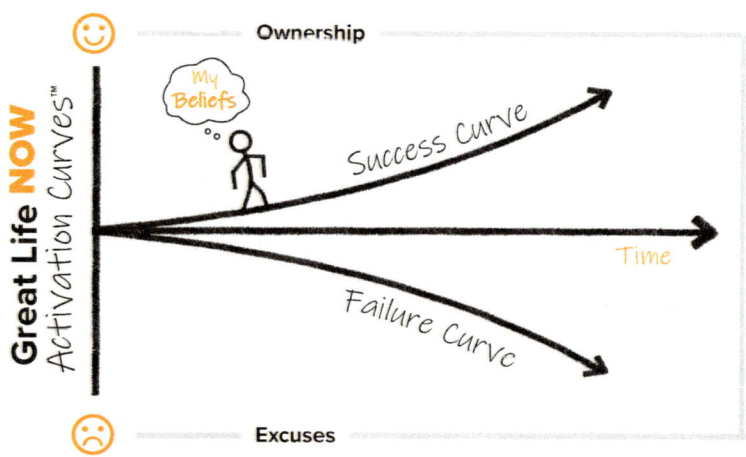

Activate
Empowering Beliefs

A Limiting Belief is something you believe to be true that restricts you in some way. It could be about you, other people, or your circumstances in life or the world. These beliefs may hold you back from making important choices, keep you from seeing opportunities, or prevent you from leveraging your Superpowers. If not addressed, your Limiting Beliefs will push you down the Failure Curve, filling your life with a scarcity mindset packed with worry, anxiety, indecision, and consistently negative thoughts. Overcoming your Limiting Beliefs will lead to more abundance thinking that will catapult you up the Success Curve.

What are the three Limiting Beliefs that have been producing unwanted or negative consequences in your life?

Limiting Belief:

Negative consequences you experience as a result of the Limiting Belief:

Find your Empowering Beliefs.

Write each Limiting Belief, cross it out, and then write your new Empowering Belief.

EXAMPLE

Limiting Belief: ~~I don't have enough education to get that job.~~

Empowering Belief: The truth is that my work experience is even more important than my education, and I am more than qualified.

1.

2.

3.

For things to change, you have to change!

If you want to see improvement in your life—your relationships, your career, your finances, your health—well, then you have to get better. It's as simple as that.

If you were to truly get 1% better each day in any area of your life, you'd become more than 37 times better in a year. That's right, by putting a little effort into making small, if not tiny, improvements on a daily basis, you can improve at just about anything.

Successful people do what unsuccessful people are not willing to do. And they do it with small amounts of effort, as little as 1% each day.

How to get 37 times better in one year.

Let's assume you begin the year with $100 and you increase the value of it by 1% each day. At the end of the year you'd have $3,778.34. That's an increase of 37 times. Now that is the power of compounding! ($100* (1+1%) ^365)

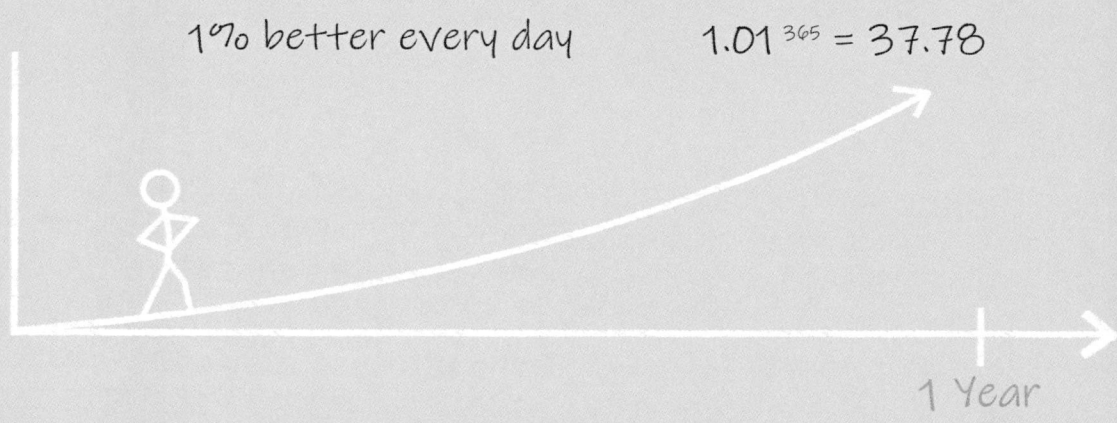

1% better every day

$$1.01^{365} = 37.78$$

1 Year

Your small efforts don't seem to make much of a difference on a daily basis, but added up over the weeks, months, and years, your daily disciplined habits compound into significant success in the long-term. (The graph looks a lot like your desired Success Curve, doesn't it?)

Now, suppose you wanted to become an expert in investing or in real estate (or pick any subject that will help you on your **Great Life NOW journey**). What if you agreed to the habit of reading 10 pages on the subject each day, every single day, for one year? Wouldn't that lead you down the pathway of significant knowledge, positioning you to sprint up the Success Curve? Those 10 pages a day would compound to 3,650 pages or the equivalent of a few dozen books of career or life-changing know-how. Would you grow and improve in that subject? Would you have more opportunities for success in your focus areas for growth? You absolutely would!

The only way to change is to firs make the **decision to change.**

Your WHAT, WHY, and HOW

(goals, benefits and habits)

A Great Life NOW doesn't just happen—it comes from thinking, planning, and pursuing what is most important to you. NOW is the time to put your Great Life NOW Game Plan into action by clarifying what you want, the desired results you'll feel great about, and the necessary thoughts and actions (habits) to bring your vision of success to reality.

Activate
Your Goals and Habits

Setting and working toward goals will contribute to happiness in a variety of ways that include creating motivation, engagement, and pleasure, and instilling a sense of accomplishment and confidence in what you can do in the future.

Are you ready? Begin with one goal.

If you **AIM** at **NOTHING,**

you'll **HIT IT** every time.

~ **Zig Ziglar**

WHAT
is your GOAL?

Describe what you want (the goal you want to achieve).

You'll want to be sure to include a reasonable amount of description. You wouldn't sit down in a hairdresser's chair and say, "Cut my hair." You'd want to be specific about what you want it to look like. If you were shopping for a new home, you wouldn't tell the realtor, "Find me a house." You'd want to describe the type of home you're most interested in.

So, don't write down a goal that you want to "be healthier." Instead, write down what you want to achieve that you think will lead you to a healthier lifestyle. Or, don't simply write that you want to "be happier" or "more productive" or "achieve financial freedom." Instead, be specific and write down what you want to achieve that you believe will lead you to more happiness, or make you more productive, or cause you to feel as though you've reached your financial aspirations.

What do you want? Be specific.

WHY
does it matter?

Know your WHY (the bene t to your life).

How is achieving your goal going to positively influence your life? Quite often, you'll find the content of your goal may be less important to your overall well-being than your reasons for pursuing it. Here is your chance to clearly state why achieving this goal is important to you.

In order to discover why the goal matters, consider the following:

- What specific benefits will you experience in your personal life? In your work life?

- If you don't achieve the goal, what consequences might you face?

- How will achieving the goal make a positive difference in your life?

- How will achieving the goal make a positive difference in the lives of others?

Why is this goal a benefit to you?

A habit

is nothing more than

a thought or action

that you **repeat**

over and over
until it becomes

automatic
and almost
effortless

HOW
will you achieve your goal?

Design the habits that fuel your success (the thoughts and actions required).

What thoughts, rituals, routines, or behaviors should you commit to because they will lead to your success over time? What will support you on your journey to achieving what you want (your goal)?

Describe your HOW (thoughts, rituals, routines, behaviors).

While goals serve the purpose of briefly focusing your attention and setting direction, the real source of

HAPPINESS

comes from the journey to accomplish those goals.

Your habits determine how **Great** your life will be. Your habits are nothing more than a thought or action that you repeat over and over until it becomes automatic and almost effortless.

Nothing will work unless you do.
~ Maya Angelou

Some habits you design into your Great Life NOW Game Plan may take you out of your comfort zone. That is okay. In fact, getting out of your comfort zone is a good thing. You'll see that comfort doesn't lead to happiness. **Making progress on your habits leads to more happiness.**

ADVERSITY
is going to strike!

Any adult who has lived a couple of hours in the real world knows this. There will be times when you feel you are "**failing.**"

Champions keep playing until they get it right.

~ Billie Jean King

The key to success

is not avoiding the Failure Curve, it's knowing how to get off it and back on the Success Curve.

Obstacles will get in your way and knock you down, but they won't knock you out.

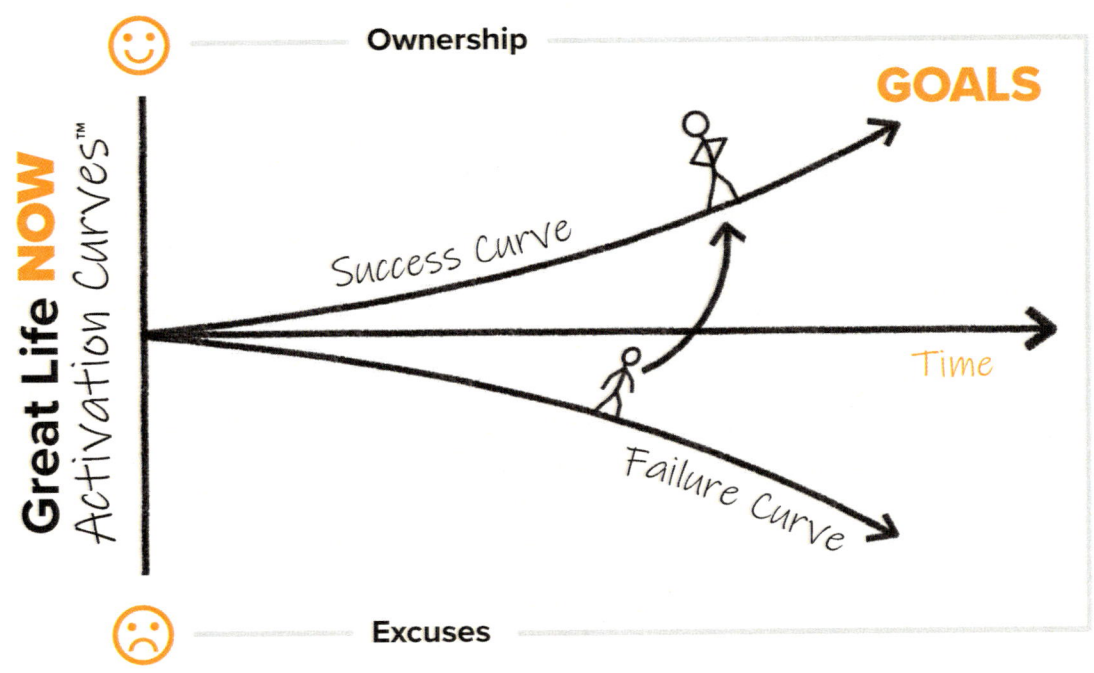

What obstacles might knock you down?	What will you do to get back on the Success Curve?

Keep making PROGRESS!

Your HAPPINESS Has EVERYTHING to do with your HABITS and the PROGRESS YOU MAKE

For each day, week, and month along the way, you'll experience accomplishments and occasional failures. Both have an impact on your happiness to different degrees. But it's typically not the accomplishments and failures themselves that most impact your happiness level. Instead, it's the **habits** that lead to success and the **progress** you've made, even in the face of failure.

It's the positive, daily habits that separate the winners from the losers in the game of life.

The secret formula for happiness:

HABITS + PROGRESS =
HAPPINESS

Once you have documented your belief system and Core Values, you'll start to see that the habits you define will become a part of this identity. You'll stick to them because they are a part of YOU. So when you're doing your habits, you're living your brand and bringing your values to life.

Over time, as you make progress performing your habits, you reinforce your beliefs about yourself, and before you know it... BAM!!!... you actually become The Brand Called YOU.

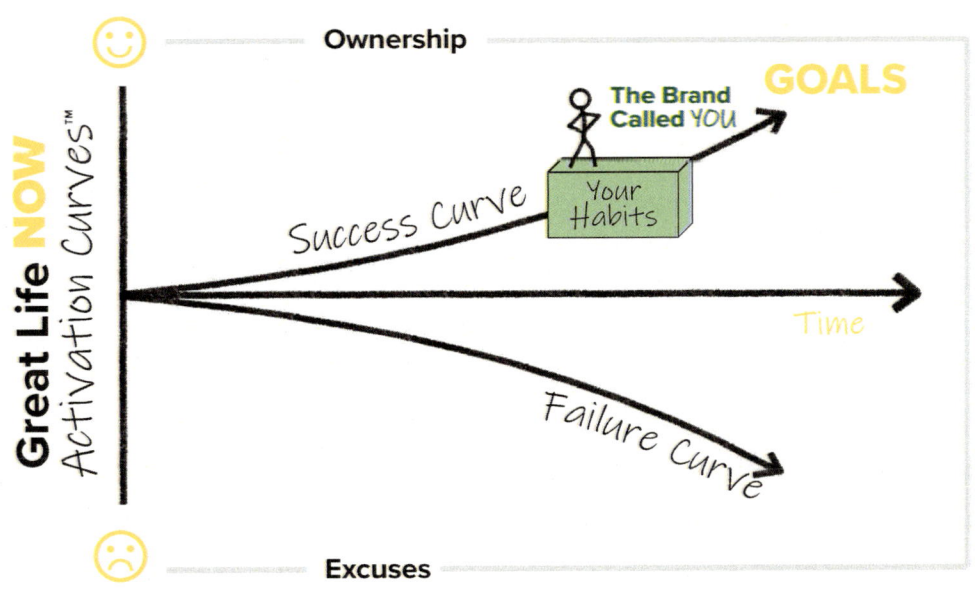

WHAT, WHY, and HOW

Go through the process a few more times for **additional goals.**

Get a free template at:

www.gregglederman.com

Activate
MORE Goals and Habits

GOAL
(what you want; be specific)

HABITS (routines and behaviors)

WHY
(benefit to you)

GOAL
(what you want; be specific)

HABITS (routines and behaviors)

WHY
(benefit to you)

GOAL
(what you want; be specific)

HABITS (routines and behaviors)

WHY
(benefit to you)

Are you committed to being
a Great Lifer?

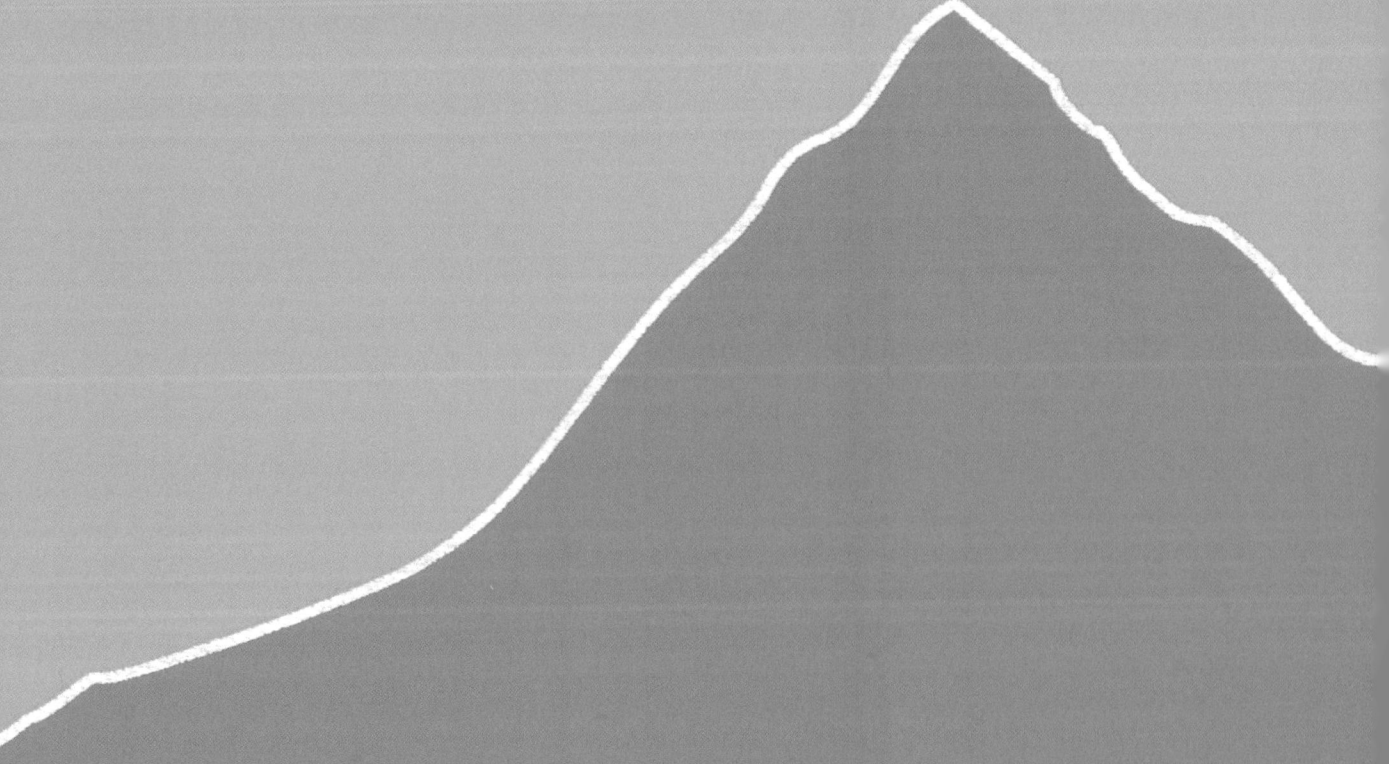

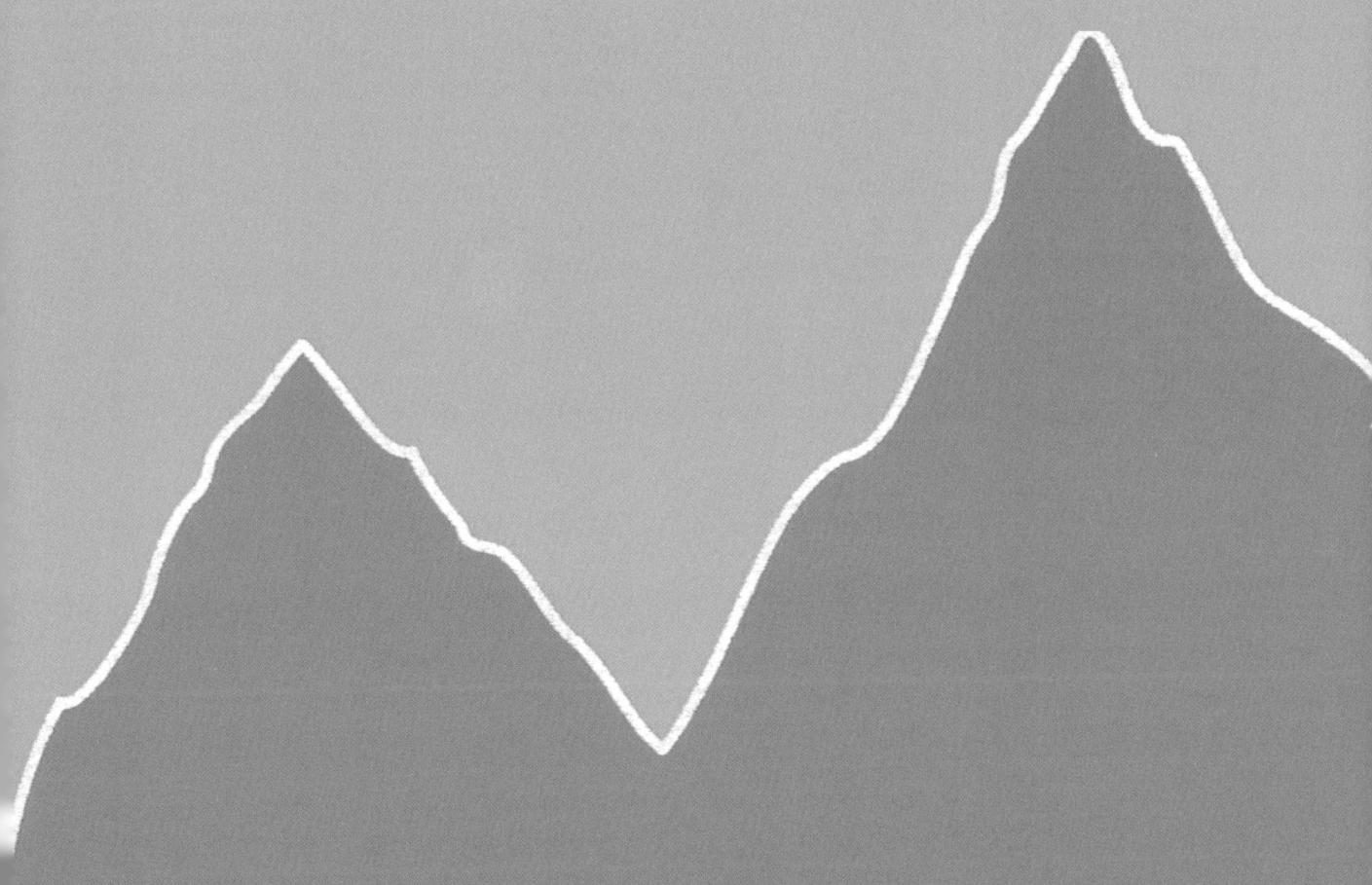

Great Lifers live with a sense of optimism and purpose. They have more energy and focus that keeps them climbing up the Success Curve and moving their Mountains for Growth. Great Lifers know how to manage their setbacks to ensure progress over time, and they relentlessly manage their beliefs and maintain a commitment to doing the daily habits that make life Great.

You can make
sure you are living

a Great
Life NOW

**by doing what
Great Lifers do...**

Once again... will you invest about 3% of your day

so you can ensure the other 97% is truly Great?

INVEST IN A

½ HOUR OF POWER!

That's what it takes to become a **Great Lifer!**

Remember, we calculated that, on average, you have 960 minutes each day. 3% of that is approximately 30 minutes. That's it!

16 *hours awake*
x 60 *minutes per hour*
———
960 *minutes each day*

Imagine:

What if you set aside 30 minutes each morning to stay on the Success Curve?

How would you invest that time?

INVEST IN TWO
UNIVERSAL HABITS

It doesn't matter what your goals are. . . these two habits will help you create the positive energy, focus, and momentum to move up the Success Curve to achieve them.

Two Universal Habits for
Your ½ Hour of Power:

1. **Meditate to Reflect, Refocus, and Reenergize.**

2. **Determine your Daily Top 5.**

Meditate to
Reflect Refocus, & Reenergize

Don't be an anti-meditator if you've failed in the past. NOW is the time to try again.

Meditation helps you "de-excite" your nervous system, reflect on what's most important, and create optimism and positive energy to get your day off to a great start.

Two reasons why you should meditate daily:

1. Meditation makes your brain more efficient (and maybe even smarter).

2. Meditation can dramatically reduce stress.

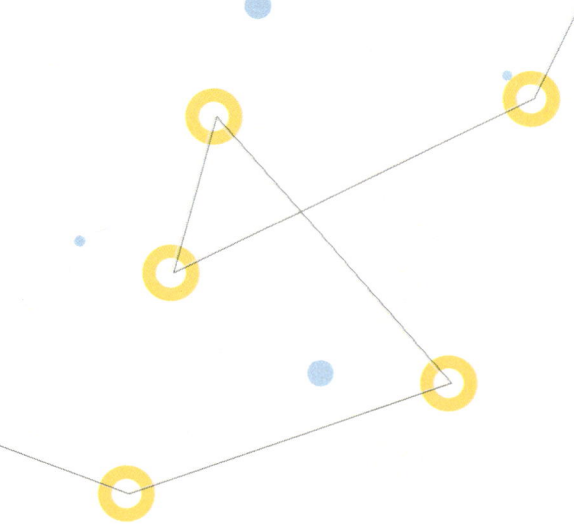

Focus On Your
Daily Top 5

Put your Great Life NOW Game Plan into action with the Daily Top 5 approach to managing your to-do list. It is a simple step-by-step approach that includes the following activities:

- ⦿ Establishing top priorities
- ⦿ Blocking time on your calendar to get them done
- ⦿ Appreciating your progress along the way

By following the Daily Top 5 method, you will train your brain to focus your attention and time on your highest priority stuff, and guess what? After investing a few weeks doing this, you will be pleasantly surprised how much progress you can make up the Success Curve.

For tips and techniques on what Great Lifers do to incorporate meditation and the Daily Top 5 into their ½ Hour of Power, visit:

www.gregglederman.com

The Power of
PROGRESS
(NOT Perfection)

Progress in doing your habits is the secret to happiness. Those who strive for perfection often end up disappointed and on the Failure Curve.

What matters most is
CONSISTENCY OVER TIME
not the intensity of consecutive days
or weeks performing your new habits.

Making your new habits stick won't always be easy. It takes time to get yourself up that Success Curve. You will fall off at times, landing on the Failure Curve. Don't quit if you lose focus or forget to perform the habits you've promised to yourself. Acknowledge your setback and pull yourself up onto that Success Curve.

Don't quit.

Acknowledge the setback and **keep moving forward**.

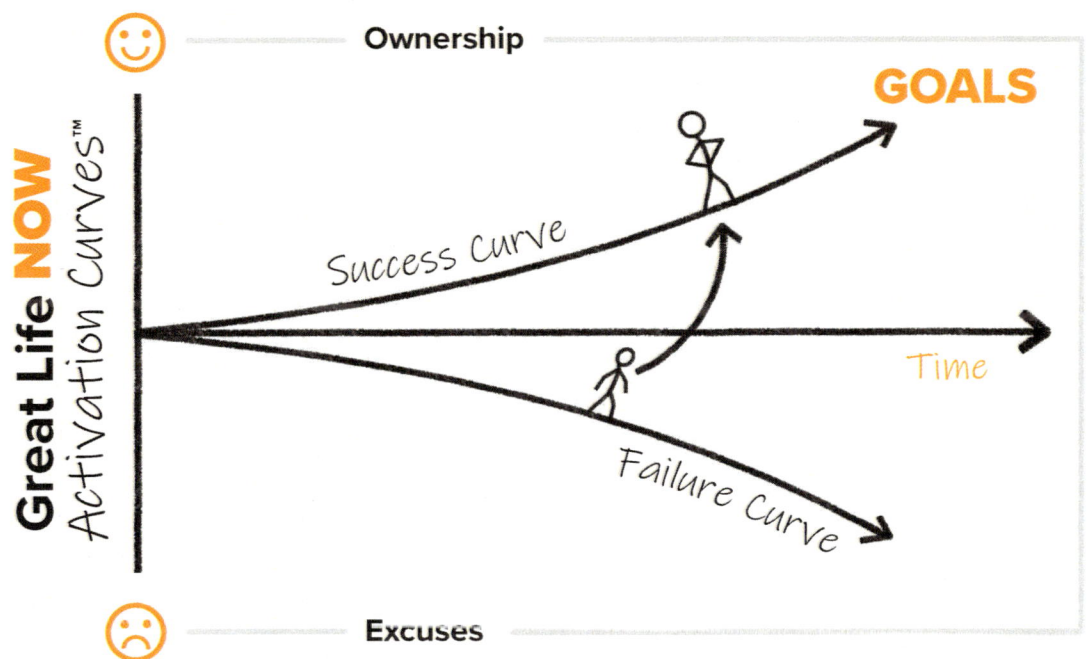

If you keep trying, you will
MAKE PROGRESS OVER TIME.

You're on your way.

You KNOW
what to do to become
a Great Lifer.

NOW do it!

This entire book has set you up on your journey to become a Great Lifer. You've learned how Great Lifers build and activate a Game Plan to retool how they **think, speak, and act**. You **KNOW** what to do, and **NOW** is the time to do it.

You have the opportunity to join the ranks of the many who've escaped Someday Island and taken control of the game of life. Don't forget, you make the rules (the values that make up **The Brand Called YOU**), and you can commit to living with a Purpose and a relentless focus on the goals and habits that will lead to less stress and more optimism, happiness, and success.

You KNOW it.
Go DO it.

Good news!
You don't need to do it alone.

You have four options. Three of them will help you implement your Great Life NOW Game Plan (and become a Great Lifer).

Option 1: Do nothing.

Maintain your status quo. If you're happy where you are now with respect to happiness, goal achievement, and how you think, speak, and act, then this may be the best option for you.

However, if you've completely optimized your happiness, you probably wouldn't have read all the way to this point. But since you did make it this far, hopefully one of the following options will help you achieve an even greater life moving forward.

Option 2: Join the Great Life **NOW** Community.

The Great Life NOW Community is free to join and you get access to the recommended tools, techniques, and templates to help you manage your Great Life NOW Game Plan.

Sign up at: gregglederman.com

Option 3: Partner with family, friends, or coworkers.

Going through the Great Life NOW journey with those you care about is incredibly rewarding, adds a layer of fun, and creates instant accountability.

Inspire each other and check in to update on progress, share a thoughtful message, and send a reminder to stay on the Success Curve.

Take it even further by setting up "Progress Not Perfection" meetings. It's simple: Meet with your partner(s) once a month and discuss where you've made progress, what challenges you've faced, and anything you've learned that influenced your success in activating your Great Life NOW Game Plan.

Who could you partner with that would benefit from joining you on the Great Life **NOW** journey?

1.

2.

3.

Option 4: Get a Great Life NOW Coach.

Work with a coach to help you achieve peak performance and amazing results on your Great Life NOW journey.

Learn about the opportunities available at
www.gregglederman.com

The time is NOW . . .

Go move your **mountains.**

ABOUT

THE AUTHOR

Gregg Lederman is a New York Times, USA Today, and Wall Street Journal bestselling author of three award-winning books that leaders of values-driven organizations have used to create incredibly high employee engagement.

As an entrepreneur, Gregg has built and sold several companies while also serving for over two decades as an adjunct professor at the University of Rochester Simon School of Business where he has guided executive MBAs on the journey to living a **Great Life NOW**.

As an executive coach, speaker, and consultant, Gregg has worked with thousands of organizations and their leaders to create happier, more motivated, and more productive workforces.

Gregg lives in Rochester, New York, with his wife, Karyn, three daughters, and dogs, Milo and Rocky. If you'd like more information on Gregg, his books, or his coaching and speaking events, **visit gregglederman.com**.

Made in the USA
Middletown, DE
29 March 2022

63192127R00064